HOTEL IMPERIUM

POEMS BY RACHEL LODEN

The University of Georgia Press

Athens and London

Published by the University of Georgia Press
Athens, Georgia 30602
© 1999 by Rachel Loden
Designed by Betty P. McDaniel
Set in ten on thirteen Aldus by Betty P. McDaniel
Printed and bound by McNaughton & Gunn, Inc.
The paper in this book meets the guidelines for
permanence and durability of the Committee on
Production Guidelines for Book Longevity of the
Council on Library Resources.

Printed in the United States of America
03 02 01 00 99 P 5 4 3 2 1

Library of Congress Cataloging-in-Publication Data
Loden, Rachel, 1948–
Hotel Imperium : poems / by Rachel Loden.
p.   cm.
ISBN 0-8203-2169-9 (pbk. : alk. paper)
I. Title.
PS3562.02956H68   1999
811'.54—DC21   99-32053

British Library Cataloging-in-Publication Data available

This book is for David Ulrich

for Skye

and for Jussi

ACKNOWLEDGMENTS

Grateful acknowledgment is made to the editors of the following magazines, where these poems, or earlier versions of them, appeared:

American Letters & Commentary: "Five Minute Agoraphobic Holidays," "The Revenant's Tune," "Epistle to the Darwinians"
Antioch Review: "Revenge, Like Habanero Peppers"
Arshile: "My Microclimate," "Against Angels"
Ascent: "Continental Drift"
B City: "My Night with Philip Larkin," "Ode to Mr. Bone"
Boulevard: "Lives of the Saints"
Caliban: "The Rowboat at Vladivostok"
Chelsea: "My Test Market," "My Geomancer," "Variations on a Theme by Woody Allen"
Chili Verde Review: "Memories of San Clemente"
Crania: "Headline from a Photograph by Richard Avedon"
Exquisite Corpse: "Clueless in Paradise," "Memo from the Benefits Department," "Reagan Ascending into Hollywood"
Florida Review: "On Beria's Lap"
Kansas Quarterly: "Reconstructed Face"
Mirage #4/Period(ical): "Glasburyon," "Roger the Scrivener"
New American Writing: "DCEASE," "The Death of Checkers," "The Killer Instinct," "General Dudayev Enters the New World," "The Last of Bebe," "Poetry and Sorrow in a 'Right-to-Sing' State," "You Will Enter History"
No Roses Review: "Walking with Xenia," "Carnal Acknowledgments"
Onthebus: "Blues for the Evil Empire," "Lingerie Ads in the Sixties"
The Paris Review: "Bride of Tricky D.," "My Exchange"
The Quarterly: "The Little Richard Story"
Seneca Review: "A Catechism for Imaginary Virgins," "Premillennial Tristesse," "We Are Sorry to Say"
Situation: "Last W & T"
Skanky Possum: "Terror Is My Business," "The Gospel According to Clairol"
Tinfish: "101 Conflations"

"My Night with Philip Larkin" was selected for *The Best American Poetry 1995*, edited by Richard Howard and David Lehman (Scribner). It was also reprinted in *The Muse Strikes Back*, edited by Katherine McAlpine and Gail White (Story Line Press), *And What Rough Beast*, edited by Robert McGovern and Stephen Haven (Ashland Poetry Press), and *The New York Poetry Calendar*. "On Beria's Lap" also appeared in *The Muse Strikes Back* and "The Death of Checkers" (as "Checkers Rising") in *And What Rough Beast*. "Blues for the Evil Empire" was selected for *American Poets Say Goodbye to the 20th Century*, edited by Andrei Codrescu and Laura Rosenthal (Four Walls Eight Windows). It also appeared with "Continental Drift" and "Reconstructed Face" in *Ecotropic Works*, edited by John Campion (Ecotropic Works). "Clueless in Paradise" was reprinted in the journal *War, Literature & the Arts*; "Carnal Acknowledgments" in *non*; "Glasburyon" and "Last W & T" in *Crania*; and "Headline from a Photograph by Richard Avedon" in *Mockingbird*. "Revenge, Like Habanero Peppers" also appeared in *Left-Hand Maps*, edited by LeeAnn Heringer (A Small Garlic Press), and is forthcoming in *A Flame in the Heart*, edited by Lisa Rappoport (Littoral Press). "Headline from a Photograph by Richard Avedon" was selected for *Exaltation of Forms: Contemporary Poets Celebrate the Diversity of Their Art*, edited by Annie Finch and Kathrine Varnes (University of Michigan Press, forthcoming).

Some of these poems appeared in a chapbook, *The Last Campaign* (prizewinner, Hudson Valley Writers' Center / Slapering Hol Press, 1998). Special thanks to Wendy Battin, George Bowering, David Bromige, Maxine Chernoff, Connie Deanovich, James Galvin, Anselm Hollo, Paul Hoover, David Lehman, Anna Rabinowitz, Bin Ramke, and Susan Wheeler. And to Stephanie Strickland, Irresistible Force.

CONTENTS

THE LAW I LOVE MOVES THROUGH HERE

YOU WILL ENTER HISTORY

Things are more like they are now than they ever were before.

—DWIGHT D. EISENHOWER

THE KILLER INSTINCT

No one can quite

get over it. It is summer and revenge
lies sweetly in the fields
with her legs open,
                              her Bo Peep
petticoats in ribbons.
                              Et tu,
cutie? Not

far away, alternate worlds
queue up
to be auditioned,
                              chatting
despairingly among themselves,

but nobody's called back. Revenge,

our wretched darling, shakes the straw
out of her hair
                              and shines herself
into the reddest apple
on the highest bough.
                              Hanging tough
through hundreds of such afternoons,
worried into life
                              by lightning's play
on elemental soup, her stalwart heart

will rise again, slough off
loose brilliance
                    like a firecracker,
and pack more melodies than Mozart.

Love, revenge, remaindering . . .
is this the end?
                    —The world pumps on,
with all its gently pitiless muzak.

MY EXCHANGE

"irrational exuberance"
    —ALAN GREENSPAN on the markets

Still, the path of the tango was not strewn
with roses. Five thousand years

might pass without a single dance, the dejecta
of great cities rolled out on a plain like dice

or jewels. And on my roof
the sleighbells of the gods, their *tchotchkes*

curled inside a broken jar at Qumran, painted
standing armies in the vaults of heaven.

★

See also: TIMELINESS/UNTIMELINESS.
Was it some corporate *Sturmführer*

saw a need for spreadsheets
in a town like this, with seven central bankers

to look at; the sweet sea air buffeting
the NASDAQ? Oh irrational exuberance,

you make me weak! Let me lie among
the fallen orders, vermilion petals at my feet.

THE DEATH OF CHECKERS

Grant that the old Adam in this Child may be so
buried, that the new man may be raised up in him.
  —*The Book of Common Prayer*

This is the new socialist brain. This is the statue
of Dzerzhinsky falling over. This is my wife Pat.
This is an ode to the Bratsk Hydroelectric Project.
And I just want to say [abort, retry, fail . . .]

the kids, like all kids, love the little dog.
This/is/your/brain/speaking. . . . So I want you all
to stonewall it. Because gentlemen, this is my last
dance contest, last waltz with Leonid

around the Winter Palace. This is the Kommissar
of Moonbeams, this is the Soviet of Working People's
Reveries. This is the new man born out of Adam.
These are the new world order mysteries—oh,

Republican cloth coat. Oh gallery of Trotskyist
apostasies. Tricia and Julie do not weep for me—
I live and flourish in the smooth newt's tiny eyes,
my new brain fizzing with implanted memories.

A CATECHISM FOR IMAGINARY VIRGINS

Sex, food. That much is hard-wired
in the skull, and in the softer lobes

a tangled skein of flashing lights
announces random lusts

and loose despairs, like any preening
set of cocktail party characters.

No one I know has cooled those fevers
yet. Nor walks some pristine

neural pathway in a swirl
of freshly-driven snow, thinking

the new thoughts, cold as stars,
that only mint condition virgins do.

Oh, no. Stay as bewildered as you are.
Fall for the glimmering lure

of playing dead, of offering the god
these small propitiatory piles

of raveled hair and fingernails,
and other things that can't be said.

RECONSTRUCTED FACE

Surely this face—generic, blank—
betrays no terror. But her other face
is lost and floating on the river,
upturned like a lily in the air.

The police artist has slapped the flesh
back on her, wants us to know her,
makes her smile in that special way
a reconstructed woman smiles

after she's found without her face on
in a river, as though she tried
but failed to save us from the trouble
of her being there, our having to admit

that yes, we know her, smiling in the clay
the way we know the face of our own mother,
the reconstructed face that never
fooled us, built as crudely as it was

upon the scaffold of the other.

GENERAL DUDAYEV ENTERS THE NEW WORLD

General Dzhahar Dudayev, president of the recently declared
independent republic of Chechen, was asked about the money
that has disappeared from the state treasury.
    —reported in *Helsingin Sanomat*

In nature nothing disappears, or appears
from nowhere. All money works

for the good of the state. How it works
is a secret, a mystery of the state. You

may want to say that it has disappeared,
but nothing has gone anywhere. It is true

that there have been some deaths, at last
report, among disloyal officials

at the Ministry of Oil. It is even true
that we have arrested the entire parliament.

The Ministry of Law and Order has grown
to seventeen thousand men, all sworn

to defend the motherland. The Ferrari
Testarossas and the Rolls-Royce limousines

around the Palace may indeed arouse
your curiosity, but they prove nothing, only

that our sons, our Chechen people, learn
to live creatively in a changing world.

CLUELESS IN PARADISE

Kenneth, what is the frequency?
    —query to Dan Rather from unidentified assailants

Sometimes, when you shake your head,
it is like snow settling
on the little village in the paperweight.

Other times, it's not—and that's why
God made the Bradley Fighting Vehicle.
He can't always put a plaque up

on the spot. Sometimes even He
is forced to settle for a souvenir. Perhaps
Flopsy the Bunny isn't what you want,

and yet you won her at the fair. Like we won
a great victory against Iraq (applause).
Tie a yellow ribbon 'round my eyes,

whirl me in circles, send me careering
toward the map. I love humanity. I'll stick
a pushpin into any random dot, and smile

endearingly. I'm a consultant. And nude
—I mean, naked—aggression, is what this thing
is all about, plus Bernie Shaw

quavering beneath a table when the smart
bombs start coming in, and Dan Rather
looking itchy in his sweater. Kenneth,

what *is* the frequency? Men on CNN
are weeping and surrendering, kneeling
while they kiss their captors' hands.

PREMILLENNIAL TRISTESSE

Nixon is slipping
in and out of consciousness. My father
sputtering in Canada, forty years
after the blacklist—

We hear there is this love that moves
the world, the sun and stars,

that makes the apple on the Kazakh bough
fall for a reason. *My age, my beast,*
my fingered rosary of disbelief . . .

It seems that something red as love
is bleeding through the centuries,

that a reservoir of silky human grease
is oiling those celestial machines.
I don't want to see the zeroes turn

as on a clock about to wake us
from a murderous dream, confetti falling

helplessly into the fissured past.
I don't want them to unload the gurney
from the festooned ambulance:

the revelers in all their unforgiving
fury, the new patient in her bandages.

LINGERIE ADS IN THE SIXTIES

She is not there, except her body
is the specter in her Living

Underwear. She is ether,
air. See how she struts

her stuff, unsuckled nipples
pressing up against the lacy gauze

that seems to animate
pure lust. Liz Taylor

and her honeymooning breasts
lie out with Eddie on a beach

in France, but do we care
about these fleshpots

of the idle rich? Their tongues
are dust. A cleavage opens

between what we crave
and what we (bluntly)

are. Which is, perhaps, to say
that our unsullied heroine

is just where we would
want her, out of touch,

the eighteen-hour support she
promised but a ruse. Recall,

Madonna's still
a glint of silver

in her father's eye. Our girl
is not material. Ours

is a wind, a slitted
sheath, a lie.

DCEASE

There are two Elvis Presleys in the Social Security Death Master File (DCEASE). The King's social security number is 409-52-2002. His death benefits zip code is 38116, a.k.a. Memphis, TN (so little Lisa Marie won't be forced to sell matchsticks on Elvis Presley Boulevard in that city, or marry Michael Jackson for anything but Love). EP #1 was born 1/8/35 and died 8/00/77. No matter how many mourners come to Graceland on August 16, the Social Security Death Master File will remain benignly ignorant and democratic. It will always record that EP #1 died on the 00 day of the month, just like everybody else.

Just like his namesake, Elvis Presley #2. Who was this guy? We can confabulate something of his mother's state of mind from his date of birth, 10/24/57, after EP #1 left for Hollywood but before he went into the army. Other than that all we know is that 425-11-0453 died 4/00/87, not quite thirty, in Nettleton, MS. No death benefits zip code is listed. Ten years after EP #1 was buried, EP #2 apparently died without heirs.

I am stumbling around in the electronic graveyard for another reason, actually. I am looking for a missing uncle, my grandfather's first son from a marriage he wished forgotten. The only picture I have of him is photocopied from a book in the Newberry Library in Chicago. I have the same book at home, but the page with my uncle's photograph is torn out, missing.

I can't find him, though, under any of his six possible names. I do kick over another stone, and immediately wish I hadn't: the very daft and ravishing Christina Montemora, born 12/12/48, died 11/00/87, zip code of last residence 12401. Somehow I did know that I would find you, obvious Ophelia of my derelict years, though still hoping that this search would bring up NO DOCUMENTS. Your name, the few clues you leave behind, float like a reproach in the amber-colored letters on the black screen.

15

FIVE MINUTE AGORAPHOBIC HOLIDAYS

Whose bread, buttered on the side of the angels,

falls from a great height? So you wait
to take the temperature of your enslavement:

is it slow-growing, like a virus,
or magnanimous and complete?
                                        Your interlocutors
are generous, the little stretching rack is cute,

and all grown over, like an English cottage,
with tiny, exhibitionistic roses.

          Will they open wide enough for you?
This is a song about paralysis,

despite your sweet mouth running all that rivulet

of chatter, despite the fan dance
with the missing lampshade bobbing on your head,

the children and their panic-stricken laughter.

ON BERIA'S LAP
after Hopkins

My childhood was a happy time, a paradise of sorts.
—SVETLANA PETERS (STALIN)

Beria—our Himmler.
—STALIN, introducing Lavrenty Beria to German
Foreign Minister Ribbentropp in 1939, as they signed
the Stalin-Hitler pact

Svetlana, are you grieving
over dacha-days unleaving?
Papochka rocked you, kissed you,
called you mistress
of the manor, little
sparrow, obeyed your orders
(and no others) between the trials
and the murders. My Kremlin
princess! Now you are old and
(they say) bitter. But
in the picture it is summer:
a garden table strewn
with papers, Papochka working
at his business; and you
on Uncle Larya's lap, a little
shy, a little restless. His eyes
are blank, his glasses
glitter. You don't climb
down, you enter history: it is
the blight that you were born for,
it is a century you mourn for.

TERROR IS MY BUSINESS

Homo sum: humani nil a me alienum puto.
    —TERENCE

Why so afraid of the stars and their denizens?
I'm what mutates in *this* body. Which is to say,

this space for lease. Nothing nonhuman is alien
to me, or everything human is. What need to up

the ante, call Hoover in his cocktail dress,
the geniuses at No Such Agency. I mean *terror*

is my business. Roswell is just dress-up for what
we are, larvae in our sleep and when we sign up

every A.M. with *der Kommissar*—so many leg-sets
on the floor, antennae waving in the mirror . . .

VARIATIONS ON A THEME BY WOODY ALLEN

The heart wants what it wants.
  —as quoted in *Time*

The heart gets what it gets. Notwithstanding
all the mornings, waking with a yen

for nectar and ambrosia, a wedding bower
flush with all the pleasures of imaginable

heaven. No midnight pickle run
relieves the fitful hunger of the gravid

man, whose *heart wants what it wants.* Nor can
devotion, mined from the years

of daily pressure like some gem, indemnify
against the sudden Stepford husband

ralphing on a yellowed covenant. To wit:
there is no logic to these things. And yet

the icepick idles in the drawer, strings skitter
and careen, a frenzy takes the ardent

moviegoer: *oh sweet cakes, meatloaf, dear . . .*
The heart's a mouth, and fuck its reasons.

When you spoke of the utility of suffering, I knew it was because you heard your death up on the roof like Santa's sleigh and now you wanted me to give it to you as a present.

I am the rose of Sharon, and the lily of the valley, though finally the nomenclature hardly matters. I could be the rose of Lana Turner, the rose of Johnny Stompanato. I could be your rose. I can be had. What I mean is, as the apple tree among the trees of the wood, so is my beloved among the sons. That's why God invented prenuptial agreements (sometime after He completed Kansas). But "the rose of Sharon": I have to admit I like that one best, although it celebrates a certain arrogance, which in my case is really shyness.

Forthcoming events are described as "a smorgasbord of loathing," a small-scale biblical epic and family-fest which should be the occasion of much merriment. All emanating, innocently enough, from a short dip in the chocolate vat of carnal knowledge, a twenty-one-year-old carnal acknowledgment.

He brought me to the banqueting house, and his banner over me was love. I am the rose of Sharon, etc.

Commentary: there is no suffering so great that human minds cannot transform it into some kind of spiritual stretching exercise or wretched experiment. And we want a Greek chorus the way we wanted somebody to watch us learn to walk, we want miles and miles of microfiche and jars of crumbling papyrus.

Stay me with flagons, comfort me with apples: for I am sick of love.

The road of hatred leads to the palace of forgiveness, except when it doesn't. Then it leads to the palace of some old crank with sores all over his carcass. I am black, but comely, O ye daughters of Jerusalem, as the tents of Kedar, as the curtains of Solomon; trust me.

REAGAN ASCENDING INTO HOLLYWOOD

Enshrinement proceedings, Capt. Ronald Reagan's overcoat
in U.S. Air Force Museum [sound recording] . . . Includes
remarks by museum officials and Air Force officers.
   —Library of Congress catalog

This is the man we love,
the man about to ride
his tall horse out of town.
Now the last salutes are done,
and a strange unease
settles over Washington.

The old man's overcoat stirs
in the dark, as though
about to cup a hand once more
to an unhearing ear, to wink
an amiable eye and disappear
serenely, in the chopper's roar.

YOU WILL ENTER HISTORY

But not as you imagined it,
sweet pea. Forget
the temple rumbling, the verboten
statues lurching off their pedestals,
the corny punkoid soundtrack
cranked up to its predictable crescendo.

And is that you, boy god, all golden
in a beam of light? Nah, not really.

Let's imagine
that it's any normal day.
You've shaved your own head
in a touching but unnecessary
fit of loyalty.

Now it's up to me
to slip you out of full Nazi regalia
and into something chic
but spiritually comfortable,
like a lit candle
and the wild fear in your eye.

You will enter history
as a line of black-cowled monks
enters a monastery,
without a word, my sweet, without
a backwards kiss goodbye.

THE LAST CAMPAIGN

She would bring down the little birds.
And I would bring down the little birds.
When will she let me bring down the little birds,
pierced from their flight with their necks broken,
their heads like flowers limp from the stem?
   —ROBERT DUNCAN,
    "My Mother Would Be a Falconress"

LIVES OF THE SAINTS

After the offending bit is popped out
these tiny stitches on your neck

are exquisite. Lips of the slit
don't speak the way you think they should,

break into stupid song, blow kisses
at the doctor. Some piece

that kept insisting on itself
will spend a few weeks in a jar on holiday

with strangers, stained and diced
and separated neatly

from its secrets. You can only
wait, reading your book about the sex

lives of the saints, the lance
that pierced and then pulled slowly out

of Saint Teresa's heart. A slice
is venerated in Milan, they say, an arm

in Lisbon, a single breast in Rome;
but her heart's enthroned

behind the convent walls at Avila. Pink
under glass, it wears a tiny crown.

MEMO FROM THE BENEFITS DEPARTMENT

For an eye, not an eye.
For a tooth, forget it.
No benefit if you cut off
your own hand or your own foot;
ditto for war,
suicide, or riot.

For extremities,
"loss" means severance
at the wrist or ankle joint.
For eyes,
the slow or sudden
disappearance of the light.

For life, "loss" means
black limousines,
a brief obit.

If you suffer,
see the Schedule of Sorrows.

Benefits may be paid out
as a lump sum: small
heap of coal, gray-dimpled
gruel, charred box of soot.

BLUES FOR THE EVIL EMPIRE
with a line by Unamuno

Consider the late *Eurasian entity,* how it lumbered
into the groggy arms of history where it was

buried. Which is more than you can say
for Lenin's body, chilly like a mammoth

in an ice floe, if less hairy. An old man in the square
asks "Who is laughing at us?" then drifts unevenly

away. The czar's nephew comes alive
in Finland like some cyborg, sent into the future

with a mission to annoy; there are the plagues:
evangelists, economists, and experts

of all kinds, Americans who read the future
in a glass of tea, and analyze "the Slavic mind."

At home, cold warriors, like dying jellyfish,
grow dim. Why no joy in Washington, no dancing

in the streets—we "won," but sleep uneasy
in our victory. The evil empire, vanquished, seeks

a plusher berth within—a red and rising sun?
A few blocks from the White House, my city twists

and keens, and someone's child is bought and sold.
—*We do not die of darkness, but of the cold.*

THE LAST OF BEBE

Bebe Rebozo, Loyal Friend
in Nixon's Darkest Days, Dies at 85

Who traded recipes with Haldeman?
Only one guy: your signature soufflé

scribbled into HRH's diary. But Bebe,
somebody even odder walks the beach

of heaven in his wing tips, plotting
whatever nobodaddy knows. OK, no

earthly body ever did know—though
they say you were his silent captain

on those slow days, your *Coboloco*
cruising smartly as he opened up his

briefcase. Bebe Rebozo! Did anybody
ever thank you for the bowling alley

in the White House? The wind at Key
Biscayne is playing fast and loose

with memories, singing like an offshore
banker *Sleep, mi camarada.* Please.

LAST W & T

I, residing in the Borough
of disposing mind and memory

★

give and bequeath
the amount due or paid to me in the case
of Richard Nixon *v* United States
charitable of any "windfall"
and to first make my family whole

★

bequeath all items I shall own at my death
or the official or personal life of my deceased wife
except for my "personal diaries," to the RICHARD
LIBRARY & awards, plaques, stamps and coins
or if neither daughter is surviving
direct my executors
collect and destroy

★

If any beneficiary under this Will and
I shall die impossible
who predeceased the other
it shall conclusively be presumed that I
survived

★

To retain and to purchase or otherwise acquire, whether common
    or preferred, obligations or trusts,
to sell, at public or private, without limitation, partition, demolish
    buildings, or otherwise
with any property, real or personal, upon any terms
to compromise or arbitrate, enforce or abstain, with or without
    consideration
with or without covenants
without the consent of any beneficiary
in cash or in kind
may determine to be just and reasonable, to charge the same
    wholly
against principal

★

Wherever "child," "children" or "issue"
deemed to include only lawful
to require a division into equal
for each then deceased child of such person, regardless of whether
any child is then living

★

The use herein of any gender shall be deemed to include the other
    genders
any and all power who shall qualify
and be acting hereunder
IN WITNESS WHEREOF, I have hereunto set my hand and seal

★

WE the undersigned, do hereby certify that the Testator above
    named did
subscribe, publish and declare the foregoing instrument

and then and there requested us and each of us to sign our names
    thereto
the execution thereof, which we hereby do
each being duly sworn, depose and say:
that the Testator, in our presence,
published and declared the same to be
his Last and Testament

Sworn to before me

HEADLINE FROM A PHOTOGRAPH
BY RICHARD AVEDON

New York World-Telegram, November 22, 1963

Epstein to give up on Tuesday,
Slocum to succumb on Wednesday.

Snavely: smithereens by Thursday;
Pottle buys the farm on Friday.

Saturday, Hadley-Smith eats dust.
Sunday's child is not discussed,

Pixley: the world will end in one day,
Not unlike this coming Monday.

Drabble's set his cap for doomsday;
Epstein to give up on Tuesday.

101 CONFLATIONS

The dead puppies turn us back on love.
  —JOHN ASHBERY

A terrible beauty
is bored, like
                Cruella de Ville
plotting on her red
bedside telephone, but you know
my cigarette
                stopped waving
eons ago, and nobody
in all puppydom can claim
I swept around in such a coat, or
held the negotiables
                        for such
luxury. No, instead
there was the brain saying
                        come in
Cleveland
            as though attention
could be called up like a standing
army, and used to move
                        around
a room, say
the right foot after the left, or is
it rehearsed the other way.

BRIDE OF TRICKY D.

YORBA LINDA, *California . . . Plans are afoot to exhume*
[Checkers], who died in 1964, and rebury him near the former
president on the grounds of the Nixon presidential library.
   —http://cnn.com/US/9704/27/briefs.pm/nixon.checkers/

And the rest is taps, or reveille. Maybe
he lies with dog & god

beneath the Yorba Linda pines, adrift
in history. There is no way

he's rumbling on about the next
campaign, how crack advance men

break & enter paradise while blasé
press fly back to Washington.

Somebody's shroud is in a twist
but it's so deadly smug out on the new

world order battlements. "Let's
slip the Constitution, Richard,

cut red ribbon on the virgin
century. Teach me tonight. . . ." I find

his fierce beard lovely and the shadows
long. *Asleep with Pat & Checkers*

by his side . . . "We could do it,"
he'll say, "but it would be wrong."

THE REVENANT'S TUNE

Thou preparest a table before me
in the presence of mine enemies.
—PSALM 23:5

Like an exhausted but beautiful murderess
I am done with my masterful deaths

A coffin closes, lined with butterflies

I draw a hot bath
in the presence of my enemies

Who is the victim? That is so hard to say
Male or female, mineral or vegetable

I don't care for all these categories

I dress myself
for funeral after funeral

Fishnet stockings and a long black veil

I wear a perfume called forgetfulness

★

"Grace to be born . . ."

and die as variously as possible
with a silk cord in the cool blue room

with a powder in the English Breakfast

For me etiquette was all: I gave
the last full measure of my recklessness

I am in the bubbles in the Mexican motel

You will (of course) forget my loveliness

If I have but one life, let me live it.
As a blonde, knowing what I know,
counting among my friends both Kennedys
and diamonds. But darling,
I was waiting in a negligée
beneath a pink and vacant sky
when God demanded Mansfield's ditsy head.
I dreamed I brought it to him
in my Maidenform bra, and woke up
in a cold sweat. James Brown sings
this is a man's world, and any magazine
can tell a girl the way to clean him, mount
him, and give him that last wish in bed.

I saw my body in a mirror and, for a moment, almost took pity on it. *Come here, Caliban, my creature;* my trollop, my pretty piece of baggage, my shot at mortality.

Almost took pity on it. Prospero = Simon Legree? I hid in a dark closet with my body and made mad, passionate—

Except, of course, that I didn't. Instead there was this longing for a palace coup, a sudden transfer of power, the body taking over. The morning after the rebellion, my soul with a single bullet in it, and the body giddy with its fecundity.

Oh, pound of flesh, mess of pottage, sweetheart: will you kiss me goodnight? What is maimed is not this suit of meat but your ecto-plasmic other, a being addled with daylight, walking on the rooftops of the city with its shining hands held out. . . .

THE LAW I LOVE
MOVES THROUGH HERE

"I would not have broken my leg if I had not fallen
Against the living room table. What is it to be back
Beside the bed? There is nothing to do
For our liberation, except wait in the horror of it.

And I am lost without you."
   —JOHN ASHBERY,
     "They Dream Only of America"

POETRY AND SORROW
IN A "RIGHT-TO-SING" STATE

The enemy will continue to infiltrate Literature.
   —COMRADE STAVSKY (head of the Soviet writers' union), 1937

The muse strikes

back, but doesn't walk off the job
for a cost-of-living increase
and insurance.
             Empire's the thing
that totters forward with its mouse
ears on, paterfamilias
of so many little feet become a constant
perfume.
          And yet: no praise,
no blame. The grass is still
green to the cheek. And we are heirs

to grace which made the tummler
stay at his Borscht Belt post

and dance. *Alack, alas.* What say you
soldiers of the lyre, we wait
for some o'clock and then *stop*
singing? Oh I would stop, oh yes

and let the feckless meadow fill
with xylophones and snow, the striped

tail of the muse slap in her burrow.

GLASBURYON

No one is counting in the bedclothes tonight.
No calling cards left on the silver tray.
No stray trolls, snoring beneath a street sign.
No daughter sits down
with a sharp knife and a pomegranate.
Let the old roan whinny in the barley,
the cinder-boy sleep just as his brothers slept.
Nothing is coming. You can hear it
in the slowness of this St. John's night
as it eats through the fields and levitates
the barn. Nothing is waiting
in a suit of mail out in the summer dawn:
no horse, no rider. No hill of shimmer-glass.
Three golden apples, tumbling . . . then none.

MY NIGHT WITH PHILIP LARKIN

Rendezvous with dweeby Philip in the shower:
"Aubade" taped up on pale blue tile;
I can hear him grumbling through the falling water.
Uncurling steam is scented with a trace of bile,
And I'm as grateful as a thankless child can be.
Someone has been here in this night with me,
Someone whose bitterness, I want to say,
Is even more impressive than my own.
Talking with Larkin on the great white telephone
I let the night be washed out into day

Until it's safe enough to go lie down
And dream of my librarian, my bride.
Perhaps he sits and watches in his dressing gown;
I know he won't be coming to my side
For fumblings and words he simply can't get out.
That stuff was never what it was about
When he would wake at four o'clock to piss
And part the curtains, let the moon go on
With all the things worth doing, and not done,
The things that others do instead of this.

43

MEMORIES OF SAN CLEMENTE

*I believe that the second half of the twentieth century
will be known as the "Age of Nixon."*
   —SENATOR ROBERT DOLE, at RMN's funeral

I never go postal
but I do think about it, how
one might lay out
vexation in neat rows
like bullet-holes or strawberries.

Sometimes I watch it all
in freeze-frame, testing
how much precise attention
need be focused
on the eyebrow rings
of some absent-minded waitress,
or the starched, striped flag
folded into military corners
at the old cold warrior's tomb.

Then I wake up in another
city, heroic sister of the city
I was lost in, surprised
by the time I'm doing
among these plump
and ripening perfidies.

What I'm doing: entertaining
dust, the smell of dust
in post offices and robot-driven

factories, dust which is lace
and petit bourgeois memories;
word-slag, mortared
syllables, wafer-ash.

That is no game for sissies.
                        The assembled
playmates, wet
                behind the ears but bent
on their endeavor in the worst
ways, a crew
of militantly average
                        cretins: take
no prisoners.
                        God, Roger
is waiting underneath the eaves

with his twin sisters, dreaming
of release.
                And only you
commute this sentence. How long must Roger

keep composing riddles
                        in your vile
Service? Oh, our Roger has been banking
goodness, reconciling
                        the accounts. Behold
the scrivener, in the ruination

of his office. Jah, I want your helmet
off for once,
                and you here in the ooze
with us. While Roger resubmits

his riddles to a Higher Power, show us
the seven wonders
                        of your crazed fecundity,

and let us glimpse your impish, homicidal

face. Or just get out of Dodge. You know
you only maim
                    the ones you love. So listen
when I tell you this,
                    my burning shrub, my
little flower of the Negev. Yahweh,

Adonai, Elohim—Roger and out. Get serious.

WE ARE SORRY TO SAY

that the decision has gone against
these poems. It just up and went

against them, like an enormous rearing
horse, a careening locomotive, and we

tried to get out of the way. We still
wake up screaming. Frankly

the decision scares us
more than a little. We think it wears

a muscle shirt and is named Bluto,
but who really knows? All we want

is peace and quiet, maybe a cottage
in the Hamptons, some sort of tonic

for our splintered nerves. That's what
we want, but there are sparrows

on the roof. And white roiling seas
of manuscripts that curse

and shriek, and tender envelopes
that bleed hysterically when opened.

REVENGE, LIKE HABANERO PEPPERS

The law I love is major mover
—ROBERT DUNCAN

Revenge, like habanero peppers, clears
the sinuses, presses the errant

sweetness into every flower. I'd swear
the trees were giddier than usual

today, all that leaf-glitter trembling
to give away such money. I graze, oh

I shall graze long and affectionately
on the fiefdom I survey, though I am

no seashell-gatherer, nor do I wander
cluelessly among the darling buds

of May (etc., etc.). On this plane
for the duration: loyal and doddering

like some old stooped family retainer
with a plot-twisting identity, I remain

the rhapsodist of cunning, blithering
songbird of iniquity, and while-u-wait

the law I love moves through here
like a wall of fire, and it is leaving

everything exactly as it stands, and
saving nothing standing in its wake.

CONTINENTAL DRIFT

The continents once formed part of a
single land mass called "Pangaea."
  —children's encyclopedia

You pumped that liquid sand into the ground
yourself and sank
those hold-downs. They were there
to keep the empty house from thinking
it had other things to do, some preternaturally calm
October day in earthquake weather.

The major posts are bolted
to the foundation, the subfloor glimmers
with strategic hardware, the water heater's strapped
against the wall. Five years on

the house has settled in itself
like an old woman shifting her huge bulk
in an armchair. Still and all
you lie awake and think how many ways
the walls might jump their tracks, the quiet earth

beneath your feet become a river. Late at night
you take the house apart a thousand times
and nail it back together, listening to the timbers

wheeze and snore. You know
you cannot listen hard enough to hear
what most wants hearing: that distant
high-pitched singing in the aquifer. That bright
glissade of breaking glass. That roar.

MY GEOMANCER

says this month you should repot
the houseplants. *Is that a threat?*

I don't think I need repotting
just as yet, though it may seem

the time is on us to burst out
of all the sullen bliss of our

confinement. What sort of tentacle
is that, you say, looking askance

at some white shoot protruding
shyly at my hem. *Is that a hint?*

I really am not looking to break
out, but rather to sink farther in,

like those perennials that each
year grow a little surer

of the soil, and for their trouble
are maligned as *self-contained*

and *arrogant*. But I don't mind:
I am contained—while not content,

if arrogance will force a flower
both ruthless and luxuriant.

It crept out of the terrarium, into what fate? Ask about the news from Titan, the weather on Aldebaran. You were eyeballing something, but you missed the Houdini of maidenhair and moss, disguised (as "he" was) in a full-length funnel cloud, a sequined tiara and a white silk cape. If you think you're exhausted now, try costuming the next few thousand disappearances. You only have me to blame. What were we thinking?

It was sweet of you to love the "air" of my mind (with or without windmills) but you never mentioned the inversion layer, how that can lie down on a city like a river of Vaseline. When you've had time to think it over you may feel differently about the convertible and the miracle mile. You might wish you had spent more time looking into that glass ball, when green was still green and the looking was easy.

AGAINST ANGELS

I haven't been able to keep you
in my life, O cruelest
& most unusual among the angels,
dumbfuck & all-around true love.
No, you must hold your sweetness
just a little out of sight, always
the veiled teaser, ventriloquist
who throws me the best lines.
Ork, ork—I clap my flippers
in a desperately endearing way,
twirl a wet ball on my nose
& find no solace in the headache
this is giving me. If I were
yours (she said half-dreamily)
would you still languish through
these nights as that caged
beastie, singing with the thrum
of his huge wings?

ODE TO MR. BONE

Oh, that's all right. I don't care anymore.
— CARY GRANT (DAVID HUXLEY, A.K.A. "MR. BONE")
to Katharine Hepburn in *Bringing Up Baby*

Because he is ridiculous
in long silk robe with poofy sleeves

we are head over heels for him. She
has sent away his clothes, reduced

to smithereens all prospect of largesse
from his museum's filthy rich old

benefactress. If only
he could get back to New York,

he thinks, marry the officious
priss who is so obviously

wrong for him, find the missing
clavicle he needs to finish off his

brontosaurus. But they are hunting
escaped leopards on a Connecticut

estate and it is hopeless, that much
is clear, he can give up

fighting it but it won't
let him, this thing is like some giant

dimwit reptile come to life and it
will have its way with both of them.

An evening in late spring and we're out walking in the wind, talking about your aunt Xenia who was the lady-in-waiting-to-the-lady-in-waiting to the czarina, how she brought jewels and crested linens back to Finland after the revolution, how some of these things are still in wooden cupboards in the slowly, aristocratically mouldering country house of your family.

Still spring, the wind still blowing, we're still walking the late night streets and conjuring my aunt Florence who sold costume jewelry for a living, how her body disappeared the day she died in San Francisco and all I could think of was how furious she would have been, how we finally found her lost body at St. Luke's instead of Mt. Zion, how her ashes wore that little name tag out of the bay, to their last scattering.

So we go on, carried through the night sky by these histories and that wind, summoning your twin sister Marja and how she wanted "everything, and everything, and the whole bag," and now she is a dentist in Helsinki with a husband and two children, and her genes are ensconced luxuriously inside her, like the black roe inside the belly of the papaya, or the ruby-hoard that studs the warm flesh of the pomegranate.

THE ROWBOAT AT VLADIVOSTOK

Looking back, the rowboat at Vladivostok
may not have been your purest inspiration. The Pacific
had turned out to be astonishingly
large, even for an ocean, and you rowed out
finally to some unnamed volcanic island
and just stopped. That was the good part
of that day, knowing that you could stop
yourself from carrying out your will, could still hear
your lover's voice cut in and out
although the radio would work only
a little. Now your voice is full
of what it was to leave the Marianas
on that morning, Antares graying in the sky,
the trade winds blowing through the porpoises.

THE LITTLE RICHARD STORY

The god of Abraham is a true God.
Now we gonna do "Rip It Up."
—REVEREND RICHARD PENNIMAN

Nothing is talking to you
in the numbers, in the leaves.
No *mambo mambo* on the wind.
No colored streamers in the skies.
No one has pasted little notes
to you, like kisses.
No Fred, no Ginger,
no sudden bursting
into Stone Age languages.
No angels clustered in the rafters.
No giants sacked out on the stove.

On a day like this,
without the music
of appearances, creatures
could land and you
would not be able to explain
anything to them, not
the fearless industry
of beavers, or why dust bunnies
prefer the dark, not even
how Little Richard
himself came into being.

MY TEST MARKET

Let's fly off to Finland, far
from the long arm of Olestra. There

in bog, arctic fen, and sand
are others who may understand

our epic innocence. Oh, how many
names for snow! and none

with growing market share. Where
are the snows that make no sense

so early in the morning, when the snow
is blue and blowing on the steppes?

Where is the *qanisqineq*,
the "snow floating on water"?

We may ask Vigdís Finnbogadóttir,
who's not a Finn. She may not know,

but she may point us toward
the northern lights. Her aim is true,

her snowshoes always full of snow.
We won't come back. You come too.

NOTES

THE KILLER INSTINCT

The last two lines of the poem suggest the last lines in Hart Crane's "My Grandmother's Love Letters."

MY EXCHANGE

The *tchotchkes* in question are the Dead Sea Scrolls, recovered from jars in Qumran. "Painted / standing armies" invokes the thousands of life-size terra-cotta warriors buried with China's first exalted emperor Qin Shihuang in a crypt at Xian. Lines 10–14 refract the opening of Marianne Moore's poem "The Steeple-Jack."

THE DEATH OF CHECKERS

Checkers was the Nixon family dog, featured to great effect in the "Checkers speech" of September 23, 1952. Several phrases in the poem come from this speech. Dzerzhinsky refers to Felix Dzerzhinsky, first head of the Cheka (secret police), now known as the KGB. Leonid is Leonid Brezhnev, general secretary of the Soviet Communist Party, 1964–1982.

GENERAL DUDAYEV ENTERS THE NEW WORLD

Helsingin Sanomat is the major daily paper in Helsinki, Finland. General Dzhahar Dudayev was killed in a Russian missile attack during the war in Chechnya.

CLUELESS IN PARADISE

Dan Rather was assaulted on Park Avenue in 1986 by a man or men who repeatedly asked him, "Kenneth, what is the frequency?"

PREMILLENNIAL TRISTESSE

"My age, my beast" is a phrase from Osip Mandelstam's poem "Vek" ("The Age").

Lavrenty Beria directed the Soviet secret police from 1938 to 1953, when he was executed as an "imperialist agent" after attempting to succeed Stalin as sole dictator. He was known for his interest in young girls.

TERROR IS MY BUSINESS

The epigraph from Terence is commonly translated "I am a man: nothing human is alien to me." "No Such Agency" refers to the fiercely secretive National Security Agency, or NSA, and Roswell is Roswell, New Mexico, near the desert site of a supposed crash landing by alien spacecraft.

VARIATIONS ON A THEME BY WOODY ALLEN

The last line is a play on Pascal's "The heart has its reasons that reason does not know."

CARNAL ACKNOWLEDGMENTS

The poem adapts passages from the biblical Song of Solomon. Johnny Stompanato was Lana Turner's mobster lover, stabbed to death in 1958 by her fourteen-year-old daughter, Cheryl Crane.

BLUES FOR THE EVIL EMPIRE

The embalmed body of Vladimir Ilyich Lenin is still on display in a Red Square mausoleum. The last line of the poem paraphrases a passage from Miguel de Unamuno's *Del sentimiento trágico de la vida*.

THE LAST OF BEBE

Richard Nixon's closest friend, Bebe Rebozo, was a real estate developer, then a banker (and Nixon investment advisor) in Key Biscayne, Florida. He paid for the installation of a bowling alley in the White House and purchased an estate for Nixon in San Clemente, California, where Nixon often turned up on the beach in serge suit and wing tip shoes.

LAST W & T

All the words in this poem are from the Last Will and Testament of Richard M. Nixon.

HEADLINE FROM A PHOTOGRAPH BY RICHARD AVEDON

In the photograph ("Times Square, New York, November 22, 1963") a haggard-looking woman holds up the *New York World-Telegram* with banner headline "PRESIDENT SHOT DEAD." A tiny headline above the fold reads "Epstein Due to Give Up on Tuesday."

THE REVENANT'S TUNE

The first line of the poem is from Connie Deanovich's "Requirements for an Addiction to Movies."

THE GOSPEL ACCORDING TO CLAIROL

If I have but one life, let me live it as a blonde was a Clairol ad campaign in the sixties. Perennial starlet (and Monroe wannabe) Jayne Mansfield is rumored to have been decapitated on June 29, 1967, when a car driven by her lover slammed into a parked truck.

POETRY AND SORROW IN A "RIGHT-TO-SING" STATE

A *tummler* was an "entertainer, social director . . . hilarity-organizer and overall buffoon," especially in a Catskill resort, according to Leo Rosten.

GLASBURYON

Thanks to Mark Abley for introducing me to the word "Glasburyon" in his poem lamenting the loss of ancient languages. Glasburyon means "glass castle" in Norn, a language once spoken in the Shetlands. Some of the images in this poem come from my childhood reading of "The Princess on the Glass Hill," a folk tale retold from the Old Norse.

MEMORIES OF SAN CLEMENTE

The Nixon "Western White House" was an estate in San Clemente, California (see note for "The Last of Bebe").

WE ARE SORRY TO SAY

Performance poet Sparrow picketed the offices of the *New Yorker* with a placard reading "My poetry is as bad as yours." His work subsequently appeared in the magazine.

63

According to the Rock and Roll Hall of Fame, the Reverend Richard Penniman (a.k.a. Little Richard) is an ordained Seventh Day Adventist minister.

MY TEST MARKET

Qanisqineq is a Central Alaskan Yupik (Eskimo) word meaning "snow floating on water." Vigdís Finnbogadóttir was president of Iceland, 1980–1996.

Gary Margolis, *Falling Awake*
Mark McMorris, *The Black Reeds*
Laura Mullen, *After I Was Dead*
Jacqueline Osherow, *Conversations with Survivors*
Jacqueline Osherow, *Looking for Angels in New York*
Tracy Philpot, *Incorrect Distances*
Andy Robbins, *The Very Thought of You*
Donald Revell, *The Gaza of Winter*
Martha Ronk, *Eyetrouble*
Martha Clare Ronk, *Desire in L.A.*
Tessa Rumsey, *Assembling the Shepherd*
Aleda Shirley, *Chinese Architecture*
Pamela Stewart, *The Red Window*
Susan Stewart, *The Hive*
Terese Svoboda, *All Aberration*
Terese Svoboda, *Mere Mortals*
Lee Upton, *Approximate Darling*
Arthur Vogelsang, *Twentieth Century Women*
Sidney Wade, *Empty Sleeves*
Marjorie Welish, *Casting Sequences*
Susan Wheeler, *Bag 'o' Diamonds*
C. D. Wright, *String Light*
Katayoon Zandvakili, *Deer Table Legs*